The poems in Adam Scheffler's second book encompass the full emotional spectrum from despair and grief to "sweet joy." With verve, humor, and gentle wisdom, he explores the indignities, disappointments, and sorrows of being a person—of having to "scoop up / some version of yourself to hand / over from your mind's scum"—while also celebrating life's pleasures and engaging in the insuppressible impulse to praise, which Auden called the primary function of poetry. Scheffler finds beauty and takes delight in animals such as retired racehorses, snails, spiders, swarms of insects, as well as in Zamboni machines, Jeff Goldblum, the act of running, even a used condom—and in doing so, he shares with us "the wild feral breathlessness" of being alive.

—Jeffrey Harrison, author of *Between Lakes*

The poems in Adam Scheffler's *Heartworm* draw complex and compelling metaphoric constructs from popular culture to allow us to see the mundane world as a source of wonder and spirituality, in lines like "as if the job / were a kind of crop circle and we were the corn / that teenage aliens doodle their graffiti on for a purpose / that's beyond us." The poems often follow an at first seemingly silly assertion only to discover an elegant and evocative closure that exists in a wholly different realm of expression. Scheffler is at his best when he's praising the mundane world—especially aspects of it least thought of as inspirations for art—and in doing so in engaging and compelling ways his poems arrive at the discovery that everything is worthy of praise. The poems in this collection often have me thinking of the poetry of the late Tony Hoagland. They exude the same humor-tinged anger at how we've come to accept what we think of as the way things are, and, like Hoagland's poems, these poems ultimately favor praising the way things actually are, the way we should experience them, and how this world fully and genuinely experienced—as it is in Scheffler's poems—is capable still of making us healthy and whole.

    —George Looney, author of *Ode to the Earth in Translation* and *The Itinerate Circus: New and Selected Poems 1995-2020*

HEARTWORM

poems

Adam Scheffler

moon city press
Department of English
Missouri State University

MOON CITY PRESS
Department of English
Missouri State University
901 South National Avenue
Springfield, Missouri 65897

First Edition
Copyright © 2023 by Adam Scheffler
All rights reserved.
Published by Moon City Press, Springfield, Missouri, USA, in 2023.

Library of Congress Cataloging-in-Publication Data
Scheffler, Adam. 1984-
Heartworm

2022952280

Further Library of Congress information is available upon request.

ISBN-10: 0-913785-60-1
ISBN-13: 978-0-913785-60-7

Text edited by and copyedited by Karen Craigo
Interior designed by Cam Steilen
Cover designed by Emily Davis Adams & Shen Chen Hsieh
Cover Art: *Sun (NASA)* by Emily Davis Adams, oil on canvas
    over panel, 16 x 16 inches, 2020

Manufactured in the United States of America

www.moon-city-press.com

moon city press
Department of English
Missouri State University

TABLE OF CONTENTS

For my parents, Katy and Sam

HEARTWORM
poems

Joy is the only inoculation against the despair to which any sane person is prone, the only antidote to the nihilism that wafts through our intellectual atmosphere like sarin gas.
—Christian Wiman

I am done with my graceless heart.
—Florence and the Machine

FLORENCE, KENTUCKY

So what if the old man
on the bus is trying and
failing to remember his dead
mom's face, as if the past were
not a cartoon tunnel scratched
on a wall?

He's still trying,
and when did we forget our
cattle-shoes and feather parkas,
how we carry with us a lowing
sadness, an extinguished memory
of flight?

Today I'm going to count all the
blackbirds between the prison
and the Walmart where, right
now, in its galloping sadness,
a bald man who sounds like
a car horn is hector-lecturing
his infant-hushing
girlfriend—as her unhappiness,
radiant as a cleat, sharp as an ice
skate, sprays to a sudden stop.

Right now, at the emergency
crisis center right next to the
gun store, the nurse feels entombed
in hours like a fly in amber

as the waiting room TVs
spin despair's golden honey—

and I think of the ice I waded out
on as a kid, of how often the world
seems like it's going to shatter,
but then, miraculously,
mercilessly, does not.

CHECKOUT

A poem can't tell you what it's like
to be 83 and seven hours deep
into a Christmas Eve shift
at Walmart, cajoling
beeps from objects like the secret
name each of us will never
be sweetly called, can't show
you her face and eyes like the
night sky, or the white-haired
man wearing reindeer horns,
mumbling into his collar's
staticky radio-gadget; a poem
can only mention her eyes,
shocking blue, like desert
pools, the red & white of her
Santa hat, or take note of the
little carts carrying each beached
customer to the doom of their
product; but a poem can place
this curse upon the Waltons:
that they be given her job
manning the conveyer as it
rattles its barren Torah through
miles of product, or be given a list
of every item they sell, and be
made to wander like Israelites
back and forth through their
endless stores until they find them,
until their heads and toes grow

lighter, and Christmas music
lifts and carries them & lifts
and carries them, like each
one is a burst suitcase of
money blizzarding open.

ODE TO ZAMBONI MACHINES

There was a whole other section to the poem
here that I deleted, or Zambonied over,
that had to do with bitterness, which
I for once in my life thought the better of—
believe me, there is a lot of my life for which I'd like
to employ a fleet of specialized Zambonis,
a botox Zamboni for removing wrinkles,
a nursemaid Zamboni for when I lie sleepless treading
the iron escalator of my thoughts, a sunshine Zamboni
to polish each day vigorously like a stray tongue-cleans
his bowl into a dog dish halo, but most of all
a Zamboni for my knee-jerk stupidity,
for the stupid aggrieved remarks I made last night,
and the ones I will no doubt make today:
I wish I could be more like snails, the shining
Zambonis of the soil, spinning mucousy, abalone
roads behind them before they're murdered
by persnickety gardeners who have a deep
knowledge of both flowers and poison, but yet
also have a patience I do not, in my constant
rushing and worrying and ugly conversational
blundering, that is not unlike the deep, quiet
patience that Frank Zamboni dreamed of after
his family left overheated Vespa-smoggy Italy
for overheated freeway-smoggy Los Angeles,
as he decided to dedicate his whole life to ice
and coolness, first making ice blocks to sell,
and then when compressor-based refrigeration
made this obsolete, devoting nine years to his dream

of an eponymous ice resurfacer, which he stuck
with, as his son Richard claimed, for the very
reason that "everyone told him he was crazy,"
which is honestly how I have reacted every single time
someone has told me their idea for an invention,
and is another of the beautiful facts laid out in Frank's
Wikipedia page like pies lined up for no reason in
an open store window, or in a town of bakers
who have just up and left for no reason, except for
perhaps being raptured into a pie-makers' heaven
as a reward for devoting their whole lives to
making sugary confections instead of apps or weapons
or moving money around, which is the kind of thing
if God did more often in the Bible, instead
of arranging the harvesting of 200 Philistine
foreskins, I could really get behind Him,
but perhaps it's not too late to swap that foreskin
story out, to Zamboni-over the whole affair,
the way Frank never stopped trying to make improvements,
and died only after experimenting on Astroturf, & working
on another ice-related invention (to remove ice from
the corners of rinks), for there's no such thing as one's
life's work being finished to oneself, but only to
others, who want you to die as soon as you've completed it.

ADVICE FROM A DOG

Piss expressively.
Detect the aura of seizures.
Judge objects first by movement,
then by brightness, then by shape.

Impersonate a helicopter
when reunited with a person you love.

And when you hear an ambulance
try to instigate a mass keening.

If worms grow in your heart,
call their number
the "worm burden."

But have someone who loves you
administer a pill,
so each month the
worm burden is nil.

Get mugged by a cat,
and be able to smell cancer.

But smell also the worms coiled up in
the human heart, thousands.

A "wyrm" is a serpent or dragon.
A "burthen" is the capacity of a ship.

Picture their heart as an
aircraft carrier
covered in dragons.

Then, offer your condolences:
Lay your head on their feet.
Opportunistically lick their toes.

Have Bella be your most popular name.

AUTOCOMPLETE

Why does *it hurt when I pee, my stomach hurt, my eye twitch, my throat hurt*

Why do I feel *dizzy, bloated, empty, nauseous, weak, shaky, depressed*

I'm so frustrated *with myself, with my husband, with my acne, with my life*

When will I finally *die, get pregnant, find love, get a boyfriend, be happy, go into labor, get over him*

Why are *flamingos pink, sloths slow, firetrucks red, flags at half-staff, my feet swollen, my eyes red*

Why do we *yawn, dream, have seasons, hiccup, sneeze, celebrate easter, cry, have eyebrows, sleep*

What does it mean *to be human, to be queer, when you dream about snakes, to short a stock, to be anemic, to be a lottery pick*

Why am I attracted to *older men, older women, feet, redheads, emotionally unavailable men, losers, my cousin, alcoholics*

Why does death *come in threes, happen, scare me, hurt so much, row exist, make us sad, hurt*

Why does everything *taste salty, hurt, give me gas, taste bad, make me cry, taste like metal, taste bitter*

Why do I feel sad *all the time, for no reason, after sex, and lonely, when I wakeup, after a nap, and empty*

Why do I feel happy *after crying, when it rains, at night, all of a sudden, but empty*

WHAT TO FEAR

The chances of being killed by a refugee terrorist
in the United States is 1 in 3.6 billion per year.
—PolitiFact

If you were rational,
you would run screaming from burgers,
fried foods would haunt your
dreams full of their voodoo ketchup
drip, stealing your years with the
witchcraft crinkle of their wrappers.
If you were rational, you would
tiptoe past Cinnabons like
landmines, keep your liquor in a
black site on an unreachable shelf,
do word puzzles so your brain
might outfox the wolf of Alzheimer's.
Or, since you are twice as likely
to kill yourself as to be killed—
put yourself on a watchlist, cross
the street to avoid your own shadow,
tie mittens to your hands, those
double agents, so they can't clutch
a trigger or cinch a noose. All of us
immigrants from the land of death.

TINY ASTHMATIC GHOST

I was thinking about how movement
is key, how in death I want to be cremated
burn up with desire and whoosh
with the wind, backspraying
onto a friend's face or coat,

so much better than lying in the
ground, hands folded, at death's
permanent serious dinner.

We need to work on
skipping into the room, lightly,
the way the breeze does,
the way the autumn does,
juggling smoke and midnight.

Look, I'm trying to accept the
density of my organs, trying to turn
my skin into glass so I can admire their
workings like twelve black holes.

I'm trying to ponder the difference
between thinking "get up"
and whatever subtle non-feeling
jolt actually moves my legs in
the morning.

How awful it is sometimes
meeting strangers, having to

—with each new person—scoop up
some version of yourself to hand
over from your mind's scum,
which is why I don't laugh at
the Tony Robbins self-help group
who walked on hot coals,
burning themselves badly
to the newspapers' delight.

FOR I WILL CONSIDER THIS COCKROACH BELINDA

after Christopher Smart

For I will consider this cockroach Belinda.
For at a single day old she could run as fast as her folks,
    though the size of a speck of dust.
For I don't even know if she counts as an animal,
    which fills me with delight.
For she's more believable by far than any angel
    & when she dies will stick her feet up
    in a *fuck you* to the heavens.
For my heart quickens for her more than for spring bulbs.
For even a jaded senator will shriek with Belinda in their hair.
For Belinda means beautiful in Italian, but bright serpent
    in old German.
For she is older than the triceratops.
For you cannot lay siege to her as she can live for weeks
    without food in her palace of pipes, her Versailles
    of drains.
For she's commingled with midnight and found only ashes.
For the other night, I found her in the sink like a tiny
    Vishnu waving her many arms.
For I watched her creep up the curve-side of the sink like a
    monk in silence.
For I watched her squeeze her limbs like broom bristles
    into the drain's black cave.
For I studied the bone-white of the vacated porcelain in
    amazement.
For beneath disgust and terror, strange joy.

GOOGLING MYSELF

I like googling myself,
finding all the other Adam Schefflers
besmirching my good name with their
local news articles about mosquitoes,
their deaths in the nineteenth century of tuberculosis,
and slam poetry events, think of it,
another me, a slam poet in Lincoln, Nebraska.
I've been there five times, and we never met—
or maybe we did and I didn't know it,
didn't get to buy him a beer and say,
hey we have the same name now convince
me slam poetry is more than just yelling your
political beliefs. For once I'm listening.
Or perhaps over a whiskey
and soda, or three Blue Moons,
we could discuss the Adam Scheffler who
wrote a treacle-filled poem so terrible
and posted it online
that it could have been me in high school
sending a poem into the future,
so terrible I wanted to change my name,
I wanted to tell everybody I met,
That's not me!, which felt great
being superior to myself,
and I'm sure the Nebraskan slam poet me
would agree. Together we could shout *It's not us*
from the no-mountaintops of Nebraska,
from the meager artificial hill of this poem,
or the detective spotlit stage on which he

presumably performs. Maybe Adam Schefter
the sportscaster would hear us. Adam Schefter
whose famousness vs. name similarity ratio is
high enough that when I look for myself
I find his handsome tap-water face,
and what a relief that is, to look
into the mirror of the internet after a haggard
sleepless night, or after an ordinary afternoon
of having no good ideas about life,
and to see him instead, his badgery look,
his vacuous confidence and expensive purple tie,
and to think what a precious, lovely
thing it is to have nobody know your name.

FACEBOOK

I hate the voice Facebook makes
me adopt: cheery, thoughtful, pleased
and false as an actor's cutout
gracing a cheap marquee.

Who'd think everyone being together
so easily, for such a chummy picnic
of the mind, could be so dull?
To which we hitch our gaze's

endless need for something
marvelous and cheap
and above all easy—

but beneath that nice veneer,
oh man, the envy, the need for love
that marketing experts milk,
making us cash cows.

I'd like to think it's not so false
as all that, but like gleaming teeth
which, though popped out, are useful,
practical, & keep the elderly alive—

but it's the casual debasement that
I can't abide—how it seems
like a glass slipper, sparkling,
the perfect fit, so one gnarls
the foot, and hacks at it.

OLD FRIENDS HOME FOR RETIRED RACEHORSES

*It is well documented that many racehorses end up at
slaughter auctions within a week of their last race.*

—*ASPCA*

*The Thoroughbred-racing industry sends an estimated
10,000 horses to slaughter annually.*

—*PETA*

I went to the farm of retired racehorses,
long necks reaching over the planks
to snap at the air, or cribbing
at their fences with long hot faces, graceful,
tired, and irritable in the June-hot summer sun.
I walked into the fields, feeling
shy as the youngest boy in our group,
only four feet tall and urged on by his dad
to hold the carrots out in his
shaking flat-held hand—loving in spite
of myself his fat dad, in army pants
and impenetrable shades, for the way he
stroked their faces, stood up to them when
no else would, suggesting a life lived
with animals, confident and exact,
like a man surprising his wife, asking
her, after decades, to dance.

I went to the farm of retired racehorses,
listening as the guide told us of how

they'd been kept in stalls twenty-two hours per
day so they'd confuse speed with freedom
as they bolted down the track—how,
no longer able to race, they'd been
sold for slaughter, then saved
by a journalist from Boston who'd had
an idea: to give them these green-
brown fields, this long afternoon.

I went to the farm of retired racehorses,
and was glad I had come, loving how
I'm Charismatic leads blind and biting
Rapid Redux to feed, how violent Amazombie
is given two goats like two wives to
shush and calm him, to precede
like an honor guard as he steps from the
truck, how Silver Charm—their most
famous horse—runs up to the fence with
a halt and flourish to greet us, like a boy
on a motorcycle showing his skill,
or a freedom fighter after liberating his
people, torn still between strife and this
moment in which he can't quite believe
this sighing in the grass and nothing to do,
his shadow stretched thin and riderless.

Georgetown, Kentucky

AUTOCOMPLETE QUESTIONS

Why do I cry *when I sing*
Why do I laugh *in my sleep*
Why do corpses *smell sweet*
Who is my body *shaking*
Why does pain *turn me on*
Whose body *is it anyway*

**

Why do I laugh *in my sleep*
Why can I never ever *find the right words*
Why does the moon make me *restless*
Why does Lucifer *have an accent*
Why do bombs *whistle*
Why do bombs *smell of almonds*
Why do corpses *smell sweet*

**

Why are funerals *in the morning*
Why are dreams *and goals important*
When does eternity *start*
How is desire *different from demand*
Who is my body *shaking*

**

Why do I cry *when I sing*
When is forgiveness *not possible*
Do the dead *have human rights*
Why is the wind *invisible*
What is spiritual about *cats*

Why does pain *turn me on*
Whose body *is it anyway*

**

Why do corpses *smell sweet*
Why does night time *smell different*
What are clocks *based on*
What is a pervert *ed spirit*
Why pray *at 3 a.m.*
Do the dead know *what time it is*

I WANT TO BE JEFF GOLDBLUM

I want to sweet-talk everyone I meet.

I want to have a silver tongue.

I want each time I sit down to write a poem to think,
This is going to be a Jeff Goldblum poem.

I want to murmur and stutter like butter like velvet.

I want to be the nice Jewish boy that I already am, but raised
to an art form.

I want to wear dark glasses and leopard-print suits,
be so affected even I can't tell if I'm full of shit

As I dodder on exposing an inner vacuousness
that, admit it we all have, but

That I, Jeff Goldblum, in my best moments, rise above.

I want you to sneer at me, then laugh and feel good in spite
of yourself.

I want my former costar Glenn Close to call me "charm
personified."

Let me wake in the middle of the night, feeling a pulsing
throbbing
desert of bare worry in my chest,

And say to myself, *It's OK, honey, you're Jeff Goldblum,*
and be 100 percent correct.

Let me be injured and carried on the back of a pickup truck
as it floors it
away from a tyrannosaur.

I want objects in the mirror to be closer than they appear
and I want to be that mirror.

I want to save the world from aliens with Will Smith.

I want to be a smarmy sea captain whose white whale is Bill
Murray.

I want to slowly morph into a fly, growing hundreds of
    compound eyes,
        and becoming more and more grotesque, less and less
            lovable, until
        my lover puts me out of my misery,
But then wake up from it all like a bad dream
        and then win best actor at the 1986 Saturn Awards.
But I fear I will never be Jeff Goldblum.
I fear I am no more Jeff Goldblum than I was ten years ago,
    that
        I have made zero progress, Goldblum-wise.
Though I have watched all seventy Jeff Goldblum films, I
    have not
        grown an inch taller or more charming.
That is the tyranny of fandom, of being a fan,
Which is to wave cool air over a being who disregards you,
Who lolls about eating grapes in Egypt
And can't really help you except to enjoy them better.
And I know if I live a million years I will never ever be Jeff
    Goldblum.
That there is only a terrifying stretch of *me*-ness waiting for
    me day
Upon day until I wear out.

TO MY TWO LEGS

Half a horse,
most trusted part of me,
you've carried me, I calculated,
two and a half times round the Earth,
to where I sit here
with you folded up beneath
me, humble hairy wings.

I want to tell you your
faith in incremental progress
is breathtaking—whatever
state you are in, stop or go,
you are in it utterly,

as when I lie down at night and you
vanish, connected to me
by only the thinnest thread,
the silk leash of my spine.

Look, I promise not to be so arrogant.
I know the gift of verticality is
temporary; I know that I lean on
you too much, like a friend
I call whenever I'm bored,

but how could I not?
You—who've given me paths,
helped buoy me up in water,
or let me soar on a bicycle,

your adaptability endless—
have also held me for hours of dancing,
which is just a wobbling of you,

or pressed me between another's.
You: like flirtatious fault lines
sparking, like shimmying
tambourines or gourds.

UNION

They'll fire us after we've been
at the company a certain amount of time,
to bring in fresh employees who haven't been
ground up yet, who haven't been sliced up
and turned into meat with plastic covers
over us to feed to their customers yet,
who haven't burned out yet, as if the job were
a kind of fire, and we were the kindling, or as if the job
were a kind of crop circle and we were the corn
that teenage aliens doodle their graffiti on for a purpose
that's beyond us, for a purpose we are told
to believe in, and I too am angered by employees
who tend too slowly to my needs, who peer
mole-y eyed at me from stacks of paperwork at the
DMV, or who squeak mole-y voiced at me from
burrowing too long into the twisted tunnels of a phone,
angered at them for not being paid enough
to know English, or how to turn on my
cable, so I can watch rich beautiful people
with no problems fail to fix their personalities,
or watch an exposé on how people are
already hard at work doing nothing to fix
problems much bigger than mine, like wrestlers
paying for their own brain damage,
or a community developing cancer trying to
blow out their favorite flaming river,
but it's easy to be bitter, and it's hard to join
a union, to show up to the meetings,
sign your name to the list, stick your neck

far, far out from its shell, so others
will stick out their necks from their shells,
until we are a field of necks too numerous to
chop all at once without making a mess,
or until we are a field of throats blooming all the
same words at the same time, the way people
join together to pray—as if God were a
little deaf and can only hear us if we're all
speaking at once, and a little nearsighted,
so he can only see us if we stand on each
other and form a human pyramid in the exact
shape of a person struggling to build a pyramid.

OBJET D'ART

She said my butt was a piece
of art, and I imagined my butt
suspended on wires next to
Starry Night, or hanging
over the starving Giacomettis,
making people suspicious with
its plumpness. Or better still
my butt on the MOMA's top floor
of contemporary exhibitions
where almost anything goes and
my butt would be the least
noticeable thing—unless it were
hiding out at the Met in the
Greek and Roman section among
all the fake but idealized butts
that would put mine to the test of
whether her words were inflated
by her love of me, or whether her
love of me was inflated by my
butt—the way my butt
is inflated from my running every
day up and down hills studying
the secret of curvaceousness, a secret
even to me as I didn't think much
about my butt's status, nice or no,
until she said so, it being invisible
to me below my back and
above my legs like a secret weapon
that's so secret I didn't think about it

as I sat on it writing my whole
dissertation, or even after too much
running, putting an ice pack on it,
plunging my butt into winter
when summer was all around us,
think of its patience, my butt
never neighing or throwing me off,
as if the best part of me
is the most humble and taken-for-
granted part, my greatest asset if
you will, although come to think of
it she didn't say it was good art,
only a "piece" of it, as if it's
not complete without her hands
on it, or without the finishing touch
of some well-fitting jeans that
she gives me for Christmas,
or as if its quality is up for
grabs, subject to taste and time
until it sags and droops with
age and with missing the hills
which, knees giving out,
I can no longer run up and
down, and she takes it up and
places it gently next to Duchamp's
urinal or Rauschenberg's *Bed*,
found art, ready-made art, art
because she says so.

DEAR FLORIDA

after Allen Ginsberg

Florida, you have the most stowed guns of any state.
You are besting even Texas—Texas, Florida.
Florida, heaven and hell are supposed to be separate
  locations.
Florida, stop praying, I'm trying to talk to you.
Your purple skies improvise brilliantly over the Hobby Lobby.
I don't think you even try to distinguish between sex and
  death.
Florida, you are poor white.
Florida, you are Cuban, Jewish, ancient, spring break.
Florida, god was drinking mezcal when he designed your
  birds.
If I'm being honest, I prefer gentle Hawaii to you.
I imagine Anna and Elsa after a long day driving home
  separately, chain-smoking, staring out the window.
Florida, it's nuts that we let you decide our elections.
Florida, Jacksonville is your trashiest city.
Florida, you must believe in the beauty of Miami.
You are the perfect location for Walt Disney's crypt!
Your Magic Castle is the stepchild of the conquistador's
  rancid dream.
I stand below your 100-foot ad for farm-fresh biscuits, feeling
  holy and ashamed.
Florida, you call Hooters a family restaurant.
Your glamour and violence, Florida, your red and blue, your
  two coasts!
Florida, you are pin-cushioned with metal crosses!

Florida, your gas stations have been stabbed to death with
flags!

Florida, all your wintry Christmas décor is sarcastic; it makes
me happy even though I'm Jewish.

Florida, "Bikinis Sportsbar" is what it sounds like, the
waitresses wear bikinis, I watched an *Undercover Boss* show
once where the boss pretended to be an employee and
offered the women there breast implants but not health
insurance—it was bad, Florida, even by your standards.

Florida, how can I relax in your prehistoric mood?

Florida, X Gonzalez's shaved head is an egg of beauty.

Your bird-lined bridges are lovely, I can't tell you enough.

But Trump and Bush, really, Florida?

Florida, I know you wanted Al Gore.

Florida, I had no faith you'd go for Hillary.

Your masculinity is a problem, Florida, we need to talk
about it.

Florida, I'm not sure all your Cubans and ancient New
Yorkers can save you.

How long will you kiss Ponce de León's golden ass?

When will you be worthy of your millions of armadillos?

Florida, is your heart a concealed carry?

Florida, they tell me you'll be underwater soon: Imagine a
clear sea instead of you, the Disney spires shooting up.

CLIMATE CHANGE

Today, I'm going to
try to impersonate an
alarm clock that others
won't want to punch,
someone who doesn't
get hysterical over a
headline about Miami beach
going underwater and the net
sexiness of Florida flocking
inland, or LA cosplaying
as a birthday candle,
but that also doesn't
gaslight himself like
an old-timey miner,
moving deeper into the
darkness with his tiny
flickering flame, so
obsessed with
admiring the lovely
berry-scrawled paintings
of bison and deer that he
stands there doing nothing
until the light goes out.

LOVE POEM UPON LEARNING YOU ARE 4 PERCENT NEANDERTHAL

I will look at you the way the moon
treasures the bootprints in his face,
the way train tracks apologize
to the damsel tied to them.

When I am with you, I want to leave you
to gather all the beautiful voices
of old movie stars into a single alarm clock.

I understand at last how the murderer
lulls himself to sleep on his sin
while the good citizen passes another
restless night,

how an anthropologist infers a
protohuman from a single bone,
unable to imagine a planet on which
everyone who has heard of you is dead.

SCHOOL SHOOTING

After today's rain,
all that's left
of the planets'
green and pink
they'd chalked
on the sidewalk,
and their slim figures
outlined by the police,
is a single hand
floating, reaching
out toward,
as if it had just
slipped from it, one
of Jupiter's 79
known moons.

OTHER PEOPLE'S PAIN

*And was it not amusing of the philosopher Bion to say
about that king who was tearing his hair for grief, "Does
that man think that baldness relieves grief?"*

—*Montaigne*

Remember her eating pad thai and grimacing
each time the noodle-bristles licked her
stomach ulcer
while you skipped across the
street, joyful on your pepcid fetchquest?

Or what of Cheryl after the surgery last
week, giving little yelps from the living room
as the mirror-wince of dumb concern free-
soloed up your slick rock face?

Sometimes when you
press somebody to your chest, their body
becomes aquarium glass with little people
drowning on the other side of it, pressing
their suction-cup lips in before they
disappear in a squid cloud of ink.

But sometimes you help just by being there,
impersonating the stove they want to
shove themselves inside, and you give them that—
saying, *You're the misunderstood witch,
and I'm the awful scheming children
who want to steal your life's work—
your house and all its brutal sweetness.*

THE DEAD

Outdoor coronavirus violin concert

Normally they hunch at the back
or stay in past centuries
where there's room
for their peculiarity

We still can't really see them
Each is a kind of blur
each one equipped
with a kind of silencer

But never have I seen us
Leave such space for them
six feet left between us
that nobody filled in

BREAKING NEWS

There's Wolf Blitzer again,
standing over me with a whip
as I tear at the cheery skyline
of New York.

Scooting about with a
broom, I pretend I am sweeping
up car crashes, forest fires,

    as I unpack the doll-bodies
from Styrofoam and glue
onto each one
the face of somebody I love.

THE BUTTERFLY HOUSE

For a full month
once each year,
cops, skin cancer doctors,
and TSA agents
should be made to work
security at the insect
house of the Miami
botanical gardens,
and, positioned in the
airlock security room
between the green house
and egress, should
have to pat people
down impersonally,
extending
flat fingers, careful
not to harm the
secret beauty each
body might hold.

CHARADE

I was thinking of the sad
scentlessness of film,
of how everyone in that scene
from *Charade*—
where they pass the orange
under their nuzzling chins—
is dead.

No wonder
the doctors keep ringing
us up as meat, covering us in the butcher
paper of gowns, when we keep
waking from the roulette dream
as a gnat prodded by the devil's
tiniest pitchfork.

Who doesn't
think deep down they're the *real*
inflatable man, davening
and crumple-punching
the auto lot?

But sometimes having
a face and feet and bank account
and sorrow, feels like the way *in*
somewhere—like a hole you lower
your face into to have a partial
burial, or baptism in the gentle
amorality of earth.

45

Even those who hate to say his name
love to say it, like a kind of curse,
a blame button for every wronged
rocket-thought or wish—

like how Satan must love to say
the name of God, must enjoy
the mint of it dissolving on his tongue—

his name a panic
button, a Rumpelstiltskin in reverse,
as if it's a kind of repellant, to keep him off.

But look—certain poems and
playing cards are already infected,
little black holes pool,

and here his big clown face comes
again head-butting through the page,
or springing up at the next
table, clickety-clack, like a nightmare

jack-in-the-box, preening, his itchy
sarcastic voice spreading like orange
clown wings from inescapable airport TVs.

As he cuts funds for the arts
and schools, schleps away all our words
in a bloated grab bag, like a reverse

Santa Claus—only his name is left,
mumbled in sad Morse tones through
the walls and auto lots, bars and
labs—as if there might be some secret

to how it works, some green cord to cut
to diffuse the bomb that's already gone off.

TAMIAMI TRAIL SIGNS:
A COLLAGE POEM

U.S. Route 41, Florida

MODERN BEAUTY —>Post Office
Lord of Life, Foot Specialist

VANITY Alterations Center
Injured? Walk-ins Welcome, Enter

Authentic Hair, Wings, Goodwill
PIK N RUN & WIGS 2 THRILL

All Day Happy Hour, Hearing Aids
Payday Loans & Summer Shades

JACKHEARTJILL, Free Parking Here
Valentine Cards & Bondage Gear

Summer Spa: Come Find Your Bliss
Vapes, Detox, Dialysis

24-7 SHOOTING RANGE
Cash 4 Gold & Need Spare Change

National Cremation, Chakras Store
Psychic, Bail Bonds, Glocks & More

Easter Service Tickets Sold:
NOW JUST SIT BACK, RELAX, BEHOLD

BREAKDOWN

The rich take a plane or hire a car,
but our power is only waiting hour
after hour at the canceled
bus station, waiting for the backup bus
to heave its way down from Tampa,
while the driver in cigarette-
stained undershirts waits with us,
repeating over and over, he "didn't
F-up." We half believe him, half
want to blame anything with a pulse
for the heaviness like a white fire that
pours over our limbs in this tiny
cordoned-off station like an observatory
on Mars. Yet drifting on, we can
half believe we smell a shift
in the wind, as the traffic like a cruel
but predictable god relents, we half
believe we can hear the bus drivers
calling out to one another over
their black staticky gadgets in a
long archipelago, like freed birds
winging their way south, past
office towers and boardrooms
where the brokers trade futures, yet
remain locked in some terribly easy
version of themselves.

ANTI-ODE TO TVS

Dank tanks, patches of shade for
the millions of couples wanting
relief from squinty suns
of each other's faces—

Doors to another world old folks
in their last moments
in nursing homes see—

Ambiguous steadfast companions,
gifters of the beautiful friends
who will never hear my voice—

Tiny reverse black holes,
whose darkness spits up now a
golfer, now a rotating diamond—

How happy I feel tonight
heaving an old and heavy one of
you to the curb, emptied at last
of blathering newscasters, your
quiet face streaming only the moon.

COURAGE

After forty years of marriage, they haven't touched
one another in years, except for a few fond
forgetful pats, or back rubs after a workday,
or some casual hand-holdings during
the weepiest parts of a film after walking
under the Arc de Triomphe or listening to
blues on Frenchmen Street—but today,
both home, with little going on, she's put it
on her calendar to try again, & she's
underlined and bolded it, and put some
little five-pointed stars by it, a deed signed
shakily with the double-dealing person
of herself, and, rising from her chair, clapping
closed her book like two clouds of erasers,
she walks up to him sitting there obliviously
reading the paper's litany of bad news,
& she feels a fluttering nervousness,
like bat wings in her chest or moths chewing
her underwear, remembering how as a
girl at the start of summer, after dancing
gingerly over the hot concrete, she'd
climb the high diving board one rung at
a time, stepping up on the cool white
plastic lips of the rungs, shielding her from the
hot metal, then would step out onto the
aquamarine board with people
coughing behind her, feeling the
quavering under her feet and in her stomach
at the long look down, her bathing cap's

elastic suddenly screwed on too tight—
but then she's doing it, whispering into
his ear, taking his hand, leading him into
the cool prepared bower of dark bedroom,
bed made, air conditioner on in the heat
of August, droning, remembering the
wind whistling as she fell, the cool gentle
touch of the water that envelops you
quickly and instantly, taking that plunge.

HOW TO PARTY

Your parents taught
how to pay bills
not how to stride
into the sea just right,
or to pee in the sea
as you float in it,
their top priority
keeping you alive so you could
call in their eighties and even
visit from time to
time, twiddling your thumbs,
tiny secret paddles
rowing afternoon forwards—
they never said
"Honey, baby this is how
you party" so you never
thought is a honey
baby a baby made out
of honey, or how joy
is a hive that you have to
be tiny and pure to enter.

ODE TO MOSQUITOES

According to one measure,
half the humans who ever
lived are dead due to your
murmurings, your little horror movie.

So why then do I feel kissed to
freshness by you, omnivorous &
particular, loving monkeys,
listening for the thunder
of the wild caribou herd?

I understand perfectly
you preferring my lover's throat,
her O-negative, drinking her sticky
blood as your eggs like
moons bulge & grow.

Tell me what was it like to
land on a triceratops
horn, to drink blood from the
endless throat of a brachiosaur.

Summer song,
virus with wings, teach me to
probe for the pulse, to
plunge once more through
the false surface of things.

BUDGET HOTEL ROOM, 2 A.M.

And yet, the ancient sputtering faucets
clear their throats as if trying to say

something kind, the tiny insignificant
wrapped bars of soap smell sweet.

Even the Gideon bible in the roller drawer
might mean love, like a set

of convoluted bizarre instructions
written in the wrong language,

but for the right emergency

ODE TO KENTUCKY HORSES

The Bluegrass State

So each day
when I feel anxious or angry,
I prescribe myself one run
past Scroggins Stables or
Johnny Walker Stables to see
these unicorns without horns,
these cavalry without knights,
come tiptoeing across the field
towards the electric fence,
zapping alive the part of me
that was dead, tasting
the crabapples, which to them
taste sweet—my city boy
meeting their country lack
of a conception of gender,
my nothing to offer meeting their
offering nothing but beauty
endlessly, the way if you put
enough horses in a state
then it's known for them,
not just for its terrible wattled
senators, and known for
the grasses they love, and that
the senators don't love, although
maybe they do—even if the
grasses aren't blue exactly
except in the evenings

when they become a kind of
Galilee anyone can walk upon,
where maybe for a moment even
the worst of us can be graced
by being in the right time
at the right place.

FIVE-FINGER DISCOUNT

Look what I'm saying is
sometimes not even the
sparkling gator-lake can save you,
sometimes the suffering at
an IHOP on a Xmas Eve
makes of every crumpled face a saint.

I want us to be as courageous as
the lover who surrenders his flesh
like a flag, our soul like an Osiris
piñata that must be rent.

So often
we look at each other like rusted locks,
the ship of our life pried apart
one plank at a time then reassembled
with whatever's at hand, a slapdash
hobo pasted on the front.

We must try to be gentle, like the
white-naped cranes who fly a thousand
miles to winter between the
two Koreas, treading so lightly
they rarely set the landmines off.

ODE TO A USED CONDOM
IN THE PARK

I like to think of them
fishing you out, then
hooking you on, their freezing
hands fumble-crinkling
at your difficult package.

       Their horny
carefulness almost
makes me love them,
& though I know
they should have tidied

you up, urging you in
past the flapping door
of the metal bin,

       that too is good,
reminding me how all role
models are temporary,
all loves flawed & sketchy:

even my dog's, dropping
you now as I bark at her,
back to where, serenely,
on your snowpile, you lie:

good omen, hex
against winter,
milky light reaching

down to us from a filthy
star that, you know what,
might not yet be dead.

SUMMERS IN INDIANA
BY THE LAKE

Delight is a wolf spider
big as a fist,
caught
in the flashlight's beam,
back bristling with
eggs like a
thousand wobbling
eyes, each one
staring blindly
but hopefully
into the future.

A CASE OF THE MONDAYS

Don't you too feel sometimes
like the circus has shut down,
that we're a pair of
giant red shoes, sitting

in the dumpster decades
later, hearing the garbage
truck rumbling up our street,
& thinking, wildly, *Elephants!*

ODE TO RUNNING

I'm sorry I'm throwing shade, I want
to be a tree sometimes, I want to tell
dad jokes to the moon—you've
been such a good marriage counselor
with me and the wind who will
break up with me one day, anyway, cease
its decades of CPR—just look at me
sweating and you'll know I'm a water sign,
that I want to melt away, just as the crows
on the power lines are hoping—all my life
I've disappointed crows, I've failed to
learn the names of trees & flowers,
would fail at getting my poet's license
from the DMV, running over the
curb of a stanza, failing to parallel park
a rhyme. Sometimes I don't even like
poems, but still like you, and I know a
brain surgeon friend who likes you, too,
though he never likes poems.
In the Venn diagram of our friendship
you are squat in the middle, alongside
Judaism, sci-fi, and scrapping
about his not knowing anything about
books, and my not knowing anything about
bodies, about his not knowing what it's
like to spend a year on a line, and
my not knowing what it's like to find
a line for someone who's got a year.
But, somehow, we both agree on you,

though he wants to run with me, while I
want to run alone, or with other people
reading dead people's stories into my ear
fresh off the press from the nineteenth century—
like Prince Andrei watching soldiers
bathing days before they're blown to
bits in a war most Americans haven't
heard of but that now seems so quaint
with its reliance on cannons and its
ignorance of drone strikes. It makes
me want to weep while the sun sets and
steeps like tea over Fresh Pond making
everything stronger, sharper, and more British—
I try to keep a stiff upper lip as I run
past it, imagining his stiff upper lip,
rigor mortised in that position from
so many operations on patients, from
so much talking & chatting with them,
trying to stay calm so they'll be calm,
if it's one of those surgeries that you do
with the patient awake—so you can see
if they can understand or if you're taking
away their words which, like movement,
like running, arise from the gray mush
of our brains, from the darkness of nothing
like God, or how God came from our
grief at the darkness of nothing.

INSECTS IN THE FLOODLIGHTS

Kentucky, empty basketball courts, night

Why do I feel such sweet joy at their
alien frenzy, their aerial orgy,
that burns them up one after
another—how many
thousands? I love this
outpouring, this loosening
of the night's untucked hair.
Look, there they are,
helter-skelter, revealing
how vastly they outnumber
us, crowding out even
our stupendous egos
& roosting in the millions
like unruly sports fans
over de-peopled courts.
As for the outdoor
parties in the distance,
strung-up green &
golden lights, I don't
need them for the wild
feral breathlessness
my dog shows me the way to.

In a children's book I once
loved, there's an hour
each night when
no human is awake,

and only beasts & witches
roam. Just once, a child
awakens and rides
down the street
on a giant's back.

How could the world not
be theirs as they are blown
out endlessly into the dark?
How could we not
love their teeming
world without us?

NOTES

"Autocomplete" and "Autocomplete Questions": All the italicized selections were generated by feeding the preceding unitalicized prompts into Google's autocomplete function (though I played around with the order of the italicized words, as well as which ones to include).

"Dear Florida": "Texas has about 826,000. So Florida has about 1.7 times as many [concealed carry] permit holders." —*PolitiFact*

"Dear Florida": Walt Disney's ashes are actually buried in Glendale, California.

"Tamiami Trail Signs: A Collage Poem" is composed entirely of language taken from real signs.

"Ode to Running" is dedicated to Daniel Donoho.

ACKNOWLEDGMENTS

Many thanks to the editors of the following journals for previous publication of these poems:

Academy of American Poets Poem-a-Day: "Florence, Kentucky"
American Journal of Poetry: "Breaking News"
The American Poetry Review: "The Dead"
Asheville Poetry Review and *Verse Daily*: "Dear Florida"
Barrow Street: "Facebook"
Bellevue Literary Review: "School Shooting"
Bellingham Review: "Autocomplete" (finalist for 49th Parallel
    Poetry Contest)
Bennington Review: "Autocomplete Questions"
Chautauqua: "Tamiami Trail Signs: A Collage Poem"
Cherry Tree and *The Talbot Spy*: "Union"
The Common: "Checkout"
The Cortland Review: "Budget Hotel Room, 2 a.m."
Copper Nickel: "Ode to Zamboni Machines"
Iron Horse Literary Review: "Objet D'Art"
Lake Effect: "Ode to Kentucky Horses"
Love's Executive Order: "45"
Mid-American Review: "For I Will Consider This Cockroach
    Belinda"
Moon City Review: "Hot Christ"
Narrative: "I Want to Be Jeff Goldblum" (Poem of the Week)
Ninth Letter: "How to Party"
North American Review: "Ode to Running"
One: "Insects in the Floodlights"
Plume: "Charade," "Other People's Pain"
Post Road: "Climate Change" and "The Butterfly House"

Sixth Finch: "A Case of the Mondays"

Spoon River Poetry Review: "Courage"

Southampton Review: "Old Friends Home for Retired Racehorses"

South Dakota Review: "Breakdown"

Sugar House Review: "Ode to a Used Condom in the Park"

Terrain.org: "Ode to Mosquitoes" and "Summers in Indiana by the Lake"

Third Coast: "Love Poem Upon Learning You Are 4 Percent Neanderthal"

Vallum: "Five-Finger Discount"

Western Humanities Review: "What To Fear" and "To My Two Legs"

Willow Springs: "Advice From a Dog"

The Yale Review: "Tiny Asthmatic Ghost"

Zyzzyva: "Googling Myself"

WINNERS
OF THE
MOON CITY POETRY AWARD

2014
Sarah Freligh
Sad Math

2015
Jeannine Hall Gailey
Field Guide to the End of the World

2016
Kerri French
Every Room in the Body

2017
Clayton Adam Clark
Finitude of Skin

2018
Kathy Goodkin
Crybaby Bridge

2019
Bret Shepard
Place Where Presence Was

2020
Claudia Putnam
The Land of Stone and River

2021
Adam Scheffler
Heartworm

CPSIA information can be obtained
at www.ICGtesting.com
Printed in the USA
JSHW021916260123
36898JS00003B/21